Reward

poems by

Tim Skeen

Finishing Line Press
Georgetown, Kentucky

Reward

ACKNOWLEDGMENTS

Versions of some of the poems in this book originally appeared in *Connotation
Press, Border Senses, Miramar, The Packinghouse Review, San Joaquin Review, San
Pedro River Review* and *Tygerburning*.

Publisher: Leah Maines

Editor: Christen Kincaid

Cover Art: Handmade quilt by Kathleen Kenny, 2000. Photo by Tim Skeen.

Author Photo: Cary Edmondson, University Photographer, Fresno State

Cover Design: Elizabeth Maines McCleavy

Printed in the USA on acid-free paper.
Order online: www.finishinglinepress.com
        also available on amazon.com

Author inquiries and mail orders:
Finishing Line Press
P. O. Box 1626
Georgetown, Kentucky 40324
U. S. A.

Table of Contents

Dulce hogar sin estilo

César Vallejo —*The Black Heralds*

Old Monk Napping

Fatigue is but one way to describe
enlightenment. Breath comes and goes
like loose stitches in his robes
as his bald head reclines on a cushion
of dusk. Far-flung students speak
his name with reverence.
A windup clock quietly tick tocks
in another room. Each moment
is lifted up on the intricate gears
then set down again:
short moments, many times.

Orientation

Betty, the instructor, says Red Cross work
looks good on a résumé, then shows
a black and white clip of Shirley Temple
dressed in her Red Cross uniform

narrating the 1937 Ohio River flood.
Shirley asks Americans to find
"a whole dollar to give, and that's an
awful lot of money, but won't you please

try hard to find that much, so as you
can help?" Betty gives lectures
on driving the Emergency Response
Vehicle, the ERV, staffing the registration

desk, using the radios, police scanners,
phones, maps, and duty rosters. Outside,
a wedge of snow and ice slides off the roof
and lands *sshumf* on the hood of Betty's car.

That Which Never Happened

for Barlow Der Mugrdechian

No one threatened to cut out tongues at the sound
of *vor Hayastany lezun* spoken by the villagers
of Erzurum, no one drove them into the desert
where they starved, thirsted and died, no one cut
the flesh of children or severed tendons with tools
used to chop cotton, no one drafted men into labor
battalions, forcing them to dig graves, no hungry
children waited under the sun for admission

into orphan cities, not one foreign aid worker
of the hundreds who documented these atrocities,
none of the American Sunday school kids who
raised money for relief aid, not even Clara Barton,
who led the first international Red Cross mission
to Armenia, said this happened in Erzurum alone.

Reward

Closing my eyes and pushing on his sternum,
I am a fulcrum, a pulley, connected to the loaded
spring of an invisible spirit who pulls back
as if we're working a great old saw, the kind
my grandfather used in Appalachia with his brother
when the farming was bad, pulling and pushing,
sweating, hewing the tree, which sustains
the soul, until nothing's left but the soul,
a raw thing that will not be understood,
comprehended, computed, counted on, coupled
with, though it might, just might, be saved.

Security

for Pam

Through the wires which I laid
Across the rafters, over copper pipes,
Around the beams, through insulation

That choked and gagged me in puffs
Of dust near a desiccated robin
Comes this high definition record

Of our lives together. Here is
Our daughter with her feet in the pool
As she snapchats and laughs.

There you are in your sleep bra
Imploring the black dog to hurry and do his
Business. And can that heavy, balding

Man taking out the trash be me?
How did we become the people who
Inhabit the life we scarcely dreamed of

When we, with nothing to protect,
Nothing to be afraid of losing,
Held each other, cried, and said, I do?

Playing Cards with Children
for Sadie

Easy to lose to these sticky fingers
That smear and bend the new deck,
Awkward and unfamiliar like my father's
Absence, shuffling the cards, picking up
From the floor an errant ace or queen.
My niece laughs and tells me she's been
Reading my cards in the reflection
Of my glasses. This is no game of Rook,
No tonk, no poker, none of the serious
Games my father played with Pa-dad
And their friends Elton Maynard,
Tommy Stallings, and Rash Belcher.
How many red, white and blue chips
Must I lose before this deck gets broken in?

Standard First Aid

Can't-help-but-like-him Captain Thomas
points out the updated section on gunshot wounds,

then tells a few stories: the child who staggered the dresser
drawers so they stepped up to the bottle of poison;

the man who was welded to the motorcycle frame
after he'd been struck by lightning; and the smell

of an hours-old last breath after he'd loosened
the noose. The captain reminds us that people die the same

death no matter how it happens. Like a prayer,
he recites Airway Breathing Circulation and Check

Call Care. I look at my watch, reading ahead
in the manual to Battlefield Dressings, knowing

I'll be too tired at home afterward to do anything
except write fragments in my journal.

Bindweed

blooms all summer,
lulls the sheep to sleep,
connects the clover
to the fence, the loose
gravel to the timothy,
the stop sign to the corner
where a farmer curses
this run of vines thick
as thistle on Highland hills.
Nothing must be left on
the finished fields at the end
of the done season,
nothing to cover the winter's
approach, not this collar of flowers
on the creeping coyote.

Dessert

The human heart can be conned into loving just about anything
—Caitlin Dewey

One of the last pleasures,
and my father savors it
as carefully as someone

taking the pins out
of a new shirt. He insists
on holding the spoon

himself. Slowly he takes
a bite of the vanilla
ice cream and smiles

as if remembering
an intense happiness:
my mother sitting behind

him on his 1955 Harley;
Rags, his first dog; perhaps
the 71,910 tons of steel

shipped from the mill
in December 1972
which broke the record.

He says his grandmother
is on her way to give him
a new suit. He needs

to wait. Who can know
such pleasure for which
there is only the word *sublime*?

Moving the KKK

Hate gives identity. The nigger, the fag, the bitch illuminate the border, illuminate what we ostensibly are not, illuminate the Dream of being white, of being a Man
—Ta-Nehisi Coates

According to the mission of the Red Cross,
we have to help everyone who asks.
I discover Grand Dragon Larry is a paraplegic.
My immediate problem becomes taking apart
his homecare bed with its handholds and rails.
While I work, I notice a poster of a swastika
above the face of a black man smoking
a cigarette: underneath, in Gothic script,
He may be your brother but he's not mine.
Larry asks if I will move a box of books, too.
"If I were you," I tell him, "I'd throw away
everything that brought you to this place,"
but I know he will keep what he wants,
and he knows I must load it onto the truck.

Halloween Carnival

for Linnea Alexander

My face fills the oval cutout
of the scarecrow's face. I roll
my eyes as each throw of the wet
sponge slams against the plywood.

How these children want to hit,
to destroy the middle-aged face
that mocks each near miss.
The blond boy with a chipped tooth

steps up to the tape line.
Are you a baseball player? I ask.
As spare as a subsidized lunch,
he grins and slowly winds up.

The sponge whacks me face flush,
blinding me, soaking the front of my shirt.
My daughter squeals with delight
and begs the teacher to let her go next.

After

*This body is just made of elements, and its appearance and disappearance
is just that of elements, which have no identity*
—Zen Master Mazu

You tidy up your father's room, curtained
With afternoon sunlight through the north facing

Window, the one with the nose prints of a dog
That has been dead since you were a child.

How much longer can this quiet time go on,
This slow motion astonishment calling itself

Grief? When you think of this house where
You grew up, you recollect a game you played

There as a child, the electric NFL football field
With the tin players convulsing in all directions,

Which in turn reminds you of your father's pacemaker,
Even now trying to stun a dead heart into brilliance.

In-Processing

In the Teamsters Union Hall,
a nurse takes my blood pressure
as a man walks up to the registration
desk and says, "I just need some food.
Do I have to fill out all this paperwork?
My friend was just here, got the food
and left." The woman working the desk
tells him, "Not here he didn't." With that,
he turns around and leaves. She looks
at me: "Lo Honey," she says, "I've been
with the Red Cross long enough not
to let any of this give me gray hairs!"

Santa Gives Candy Canes to the Children of Vinland Elementary School

At the end of the day Santa had
to give away even the broken candy
canes from the bottom of his bag
to the children in the final classroom.
He's drenched in sweat,
and his suit needs dry cleaning.
"I don't believe in Santa Claus,"
one girl says. The teacher looks as if
she believes in corporal punishment.
The children talk and gather closer.
This is no job for an agoraphobic.
"Yeah, kid," the reasonable
Santa calmly responds,
"I have days like that myself.
Do you believe in candy canes?"

The Sentinel Plan of Salt Lake City
found poem

is a sound and dependable policy
that will help pay the last expenses
and funeral costs for any member
of the family when death occurs.
Funeral costs often make death
a double tragedy by burdening
the family with additional costs
at the very time they are grieving
the loss of their loved one.
Time and experience have proven
this low-cost protection to be the most
practical means of meeting
these expenses when they arise.
Should this letter arrive at a time
of misfortune in your home,
we sincerely apologize.

Melody

John and I look at the upright piano.
"Hell," he says, "we can do it."

The strange thing is I believe him.
With a little rope we could move

a battleship. "Next time," he says,
"we'll probably get the floor safe."

The moment we sling the ropes,
the piano, if it had ever been in tune

goes out of tune, playing Charles Ives'
chords with every bump.

The Chapel of Each Day

There were days when the wind blew
sweet all the way from Canada, and the smell
of the plowed fields and the silage seemed
to be coming from my own lean body.
Early in the morning, traveling east,
the sun rising on the flat horizon dazzled me
like the thought of having a child. Sometimes
I'd stop for bacon and eggs with coffee, cream
and sugar. I felt I could drink, Paul Bunyon-like,
the whole pot. Once I bought potatoes from a farmer
in the parking lot. He said to his young son,
"Now this is what we like to see—a hungry man,"
as he gave my change in onions.

Drought

The reservoirs give up old stumps,
leaving persimmons, oranges
and reason to a world without

cause and effect, the perfidy of nature.
Who wouldn't be a little suspicious?
The phone rings in the middle

of the night. Neither of us says a word.
Old girlfriends get married years ago.
French films proclaim this is cosmopolitan,

but French films also say it should be
snowing on my birthday. Garnet
is the stone for January, a labial red,

the color of persimmons, a most
fastidious tree, a crooked ladder
leaning against the empty sky.

Volunteer of the Month

The sense of a separate self is only a shadow cast by grammar
—Wittgenstein

We put the box springs
on top of the truck's cab,
but I forget the rope,
so Ron reaches out
the passenger window
and grabs one side
and I grab the other side
while driving the four blocks.
The wind is strong out
of the north northwest,
but we make it. Unloading
at 10th and D, I stop to help
four high school girls change
a flat tire. Cumulonimbus
to the west. Wind in my face.
Still daylight when we finish.

Dreaming in Front of the Fireplace

A desire content with contemplation
—Donna George Storey

A dark woman touches my shoulder
and tells me to follow her.
My legs ache and I can hardly lift
my arms. I do as she says,
past the bear pawing through the kitchen
garbage and the leaves spilling
from the gutters, to a small room
with holiday lights. The wood smells
like seasoned oak. There's not enough room
to properly lie down. My cock and balls
look like two onions in a mesh poke
hanging from a nail in the wall.
I try to remember how to spell the word
that means a fool-the-eye painting.

Pink Rose Urn
for Sally

The organs of the senses—sclera, cochlea, epidermis,
ethmoid and papillae—like the rest of the body reduced
to ashes as unremarkable as black and white photos
of places you've never been. In California the taps
are running dry. Records for heat fall each month.
People you never met debate whether swimming pools
actually conserve more water than grassy lawns. But
from now on wet or dry, boom or bust, feast or famine

are all the same—this world no longer has a hold on you.
And if you had too few triumphs, at least claim this:
you used up everything and left nothing, no desires,
no dreams, no explanations nor apologies, no letters,
diaries or poems, no dog waiting by the door, no plot
of earth, no physical body susceptible to corruption.

Department of Health

We enter your house through the door
with the plastic wreath and note
the rotting food, the stacks of newspapers,
the bottles of pills, and the bucket
you use to dump your piss and shit
off the front porch. You forget there
are neighbors who are worried.
You must know we have come
to clean up for the sake of public health.
We are sincerely sorry it has to be this way.
We listen to your voice which, with each
slurred word, forgets what you want to say.

A Bird Watches an Ornithologist

There he is again! A camera,
A notepad, a reference book

Occupying him as deeply
As my call to the wife.

It's a private conversation!
Let's have a little respect!

Do I creep outside his bedroom?
Do I follow his trips to the store

For butter and eggs?
He just translates what I say

Into the only language he knows,
Signing hand to mouth.

I suspect it has something
To do with tone and rhythm.

You have to speak up in the city.
He becomes absolutely still,

With a certain urgency, when I hop
From one branch to another,

Or when I ferret out a beetle.
He seems more excited than I am.

Even so, I enjoy his attention.
Some days, before it rains,

For example, or just after,
I feel as if I'm the only

Tree clinger on the last tree

On Earth. And at times,

When I watch him watching me,
I feel something like envy

For his enthusiasm.

Eternity

In the Google Earth image of my parents' house,
it's always a green and sunny August.

The shadows on the front yard are as sharp
as if they've been drawn by an Etch-A-Sketch.

Their pickup's gone this morning. More than likely
they're at Dunkin' Donuts meeting their retired

friends, Bill, the fireman, George and Sally,
the teachers. If they have good batteries for their

hearing aids, they might listen to something
about the weather as they sip their coffee.

If not, they're nodding and saying, yeah, yeah.
Trash cans line the road, so it's Friday morning.

In the house, the cats Peanut and Princess are napping.
There's nothing on the front porch, which means the

groceries have yet to be delivered; silently I remind
them to be careful when they stoop to pick up the bags.

Working with Ambrose Bierce

He talks incessantly as we load the appliances,
then the beds, the fold-away couch, the tables,
the chairs, box after box of guess-what's-in-there.
He tells me that *love is a temporary insanity*

cured by marriage; how birth, the first and direst
of all disasters, leads to politics which is a strife
of interests masquerading as a contest of principles,
or put another way, *the conduct of public affairs*

for private advantage. While we're in the house
someone blocks our truck with a Mazda.
Who knows where the driver's gone off to?
I motion Bierce over. Grabbing the bumper

with our gloved hands, we lift the car
and slide the front end into the grass, then do
the same thing with the back end. Rubbing his left
shoulder as we drive away, he stares silently at me.

Not a Mont Blanc
for Phil

Admittedly, a Mont Blanc is exquisite.
Turning one upside down, you don't expect

to see in its green promise of prosperity
a disappearing bikini. I prefer pens picked up

in parking lots, empty classrooms, silent hallways.
These pens announce with little fanfare ventures like

Henry's Waterproofing, Primo's Xotic Dancers,
and Choice Hotels. A few offer advice: Don't Drink

and Drive! or RE-ELECT JOHN K. BLACKBURN.
Many of them have phone numbers I will never call.

The lines of ink from these pens often begin with great
enthusiasm and just as often end in tentative scribbles.

These pens accrue like compound interest. The oldest
remains the most enigmatic, a fat red and black pen

that advertises and advises nothing; it took a year
to discover its spring-loaded scroll with a color photo

of a blonde woman fellating a hairy man
with spaces for names and addresses below.

No Turning Back
for Pam

The dandelions surrender to Weed and Feed.
Not so the vines which colonize whatever

they touch. With all my might I pull their roots
out of the ground, dirt sticking to my forearms,

flicking into my eyes, my mouth, when all at once
there's the softball my daughter lost when

she was a child, settled in the middle of thin
bamboo plants, the stitches rotted away to reveal

the inner kapok threads. How many times over
the years have I thought of the ball, how it simply

disappeared, lost like the names of acquaintances?
Don't worry so much, my wife tells me, her face

and mine weathering like the skin of the ball.
In the tangle of neurons and synapses, year

after year holding less and less to worry about,
at this moment I know she is absolutely right.

The Marx Brothers Perform at the Labor Co-op

As we wrestle the washing machine
into place, the boy points at us
and begins to laugh. All at once
I see myself as Chico, Jim as
the handsome Zeppo, and this boy,
ignoring his mother's earnest
Margaret Dumont efforts
to quiet him, becomes Groucho,
the Grand Master orchestrating
our hip to hip dance with the
Maytag, a speechless Harpo.
Suddenly, we are all laughing.

Porn Stars of the 1980s

The grand houses of stone and mortar
seemed to sprout from the hillsides
and cling to the thin soil over rock
as olive trees often do. If fire or mud

claimed one now and then,
these misfortunes, always off-screen,
were of little consequence compared
to the pleasure of being far away

from disapproving relations.
The seasons were mild, spring came
early in this land of fellow exiles
where they kissed the throats and bare

breasts of strangers, licked cocks smooth
as fish bones leading to the curves
of the inner thigh, where they opened
their mouths and got paid.

Estate

Everything's paid off in full: the hospital, the nursing
home, the pharmacy, the insurance company. Here are
my father's pay stubs, the TWA and Pan Am stock certificates.
Here's the police report of my brother's death describing
marijuana, gunshot wounds, witness statements. I shred

all of it—especially January 18, 1982, that frozen night,
the police knocking at the door, moving the Vega's
battery from the kitchen heat register to under the hood,
driving in the snow and ice to St. Joseph's, identifying
Ernie's body, how his half-open eyes seemed otherworldly blue,

the small fleck of dried blood at the corner of his mouth,
how white his teeth looked under the light. Cops, doctors,
nurse's aides, lawyers, hospice caregivers all bagged on the
curb. From now on, even if my dog is the only one listening,
there are no stories other than the ones I choose to tell.

All Trucks Enter the Inspection Area 500 Feet

My father asks if I'm going to stop.
I think about it. As we get closer,
I see the inspection team consists
of one guy in a South Dakota
Department of Transportation van.
By now we've stopped at every
Texaco station, and we know one
taillight is out on the Red Cross ERV.
"We're on official business," I say
a little apprehensively. We wave
as we pass by. The inspector waves
in return. My father and I look
at each other, shrug and laugh.

The Ornithology of Skin

She hikes up the back of her blouse
to reveal a tattoo of birds just
above her buttocks. This bar is getting
even more interesting. It's not poetry,
but I want to impress her and her friends,
which is, of course, a mistake:
"This one's an Acorn Woodpecker,
here's a Red-Shafted Northern Flicker,

there a Belted Kingfisher, let's see,
a male and a female Western Tanager,
a very rare Black-headed Grosbeak,
and—can it be?—a Mountain Chickadee!"
She's dumbstruck for a moment,
then she slurs, "They're all ravens, asshole!"

Work Detail

One of the prisoners
from the parish jail,

helping unload a Walmart
semi full of bleach

at the Red Cross service center,
says to another prisoner,

"That box ain't as heavy
as your old lady. Pick it up!"

Bearded Dragon Lizard

Backbone tines interlocking
like the fingertips

of the left and right hands,
you observe a thorny world.

Tan on tan you blend
into your glass case filled

with cacti and indifference.
How Christ-like you confront

everything with stillness.
What there is comes to you,

the crickets and the lettuce,
the curious tourists

bending down to touch
the glass—

each face seems to ask,
what more is there?

Welding
for Tony Thomas

As your father taught,
you prepare the metal
to receive the arc.
The wire brush, the slag
hammer and the grinder

brighten the surfaces
to be joined. Now his
tools belong to you,
and with them you inherit
what he left unfinished:

the log splitter's hydraulic
arm which again snaps
from its mounting bracket
with the last cord of oak.
This is perhaps how you

and your father loved
each other best:
using the welder's skill
to repair a machine that splits
logs into firewood.

The Sadness of Flooded Towns

With the mosquitoes,
I walk forty-five minutes.
Next to a church,
a man three times my age

comes from across the street
to ask my name, says his
is Joe. "Where're you from?
Come by train? Do you have

a quarter?" and before
I can answer, he says,
"Of course not.
You're broke like me."

The Teacher

It is time the stone made an effort to flower
—Paul Celan

The teacher enters your home and goes straight
to the kitchen. She makes herself a tomato
and mayonnaise sandwich and pours a glass of milk.
She looks for a piece of cake or perhaps a cookie as well.
The teacher eats slowly at your dining room table,

enjoying above all the quiet. When she's finished eating,
the teacher brushes her teeth, mumbles something
to herself that you can't quite make out. She finds
every book and magazine in the house. She empties
your bookshelves, clears the books from the bedside table

and places them in a stack beside the couch,
next to the window, where the light is best.
Then she looks at you, and the pile of books,
at the pile of books and you. She will stand there
until you realize the only way to make her leave.

Sonogram Shows Dying Twin Holding His Sister's Hand in the Womb
after an Associated Press news article

The muffled noises through the amniotic fluid
sometimes make her smile, the dub dub dub
of a bass line, the ha ha ha from a punchline,
though sometimes the sounds are of a different
nature, the gasping Nooo, the rasping wheeze,
those sharp, jerking inhalations. She often
does not know whether all is well or safe.
What does she know? The world is imperfect
and competitive. She will have to fight for every
bite, for every affectionate caress, every delighted
glance. Nothing is perfectible. If not in the womb
then where is the seed of original sin planted?
Can there ever be enough love to go around?
With one hand she holds the hand of her brother;
with the other, she squeezes his throat.

After the Fire

On the wall of the kitchen hang maybe twenty old-fashioned
hand-crank mixers. "Quite a collection you've got here,"
I offer to Lois while Skip fills out the forms for emergency
food and clothing—$110.00 for each family member.
Now she's up from her chair, coming out of her astonishment,
thinking to herself how it could have been worse. She shows
me the oldest, patented in 1915. "So many cakes," she says,
turning the handle, whisking the smell of smoke in a bevel of motion.

For Susan, Killed in a Car Accident near the River Jordan

Walking to work, I think my God. I step through puddles
after last night's rain, and turning to look at my boot prints
on the concrete, I think oh my God. I see a bumper sticker
on a dirty car proclaiming I should fear God and no one else,

and I think my God. I squint at sunlight reflecting off a window.
I open my office door and imagine the moment when I will take off
the nameplate, and I think, my God. I listen to my colleague
in an adjacent office as he talks to a student about the difference

between music on albums and music on CDs, between the words
audience and *crowd,* and I think, my God. The phone rings,
my hand pausing in mid-reach. I glance at the books on the shelves,
and I think, my God. Pam asks if she should stop by with Iris before

my night class, and before I can answer I think, my God. Someone
says Wow! to someone else out of sight. People stand outside
my window to smoke. Coffee in the cup warms my hand. I think
my God, I want to go home, hug my wife and my daughter. I want

to eat popcorn with them after the workday's done and watch
a silly movie. I want to re-read Robert Leckie, the part when
he's in a foxhole on Guadalcanal and looks at the oval sky,
then calls palm trees giant asterisks. Ma Joad comes to mind,

the scene where she burns in a little coal stove all the charming
postcards and photos and letters which she can't take to California,
and I think, my God. I close the door, put my head down on the desk
as if I were in grade school again, and I think my God, my God.

Rhetoric
after Jan Beatty

Writing becomes writting. Commitment becomes committment.
Over the years, I have seen this a time or two. *Before I can grade*

your paper, I explain, *please go over it again and use the spell
check. Oh, I didn't write it*, she replies. Now this I'm hearing

for the first time. *Your name is on the paper. Is this your paper?*
She says yes. *Then what do you mean you didn't write this?*

She did, the student says. I look around. We're the only two
in my office. I have someone waiting in the hallway, and a full

roster of students to see today. Trying not to sound like Abbott
and Costello, I ask, *Who wrote the paper then?* She says, *She did.*

Well, who's she? The student rolls her eyes and looks at me
as if to say I have failed to understand the nature of exasperation,

as if my own life has been a binary of simply yes and no.
My other, she says. *Your other? Where's your other?* I ask.

She's inside me, she answers. We look at each other without
saying a word. Suddenly I realize she's absolutely serious.

There will be time for referrals, time for getting the right
assistance to where it is needed, but for now I need

to be serious, too. Slowly, carefully, I say, *Tell your other
to get a dictionary, then afterward bring the paper to me again.*

The Spillway at the Mansfield Dam

Out over the top
go the local newspapers,

maps, cell phones,
aspirin, my perfect

120/80 blood pressure,
fire ants, mobile homes,

junked cars, computers,
trees, washing machines,

Motorolas, photographs
of strangers, teddy bears,

gas cylinders, apples, oranges,
cups of coffee, granola bars,

beer, T-shirts, the wheat crop,
plastic milk jugs, water tanks,

cookware and crockery—
while under the brown glare

of a streetlight, more rain
comes down in blurry lines.

Practice
for Iris

Steam rises from the heated pool behind
the goal. Each girl bounces a ball on one
knee, and then the next, between the red cones.
Right now this is the most important thing
in the world: white steam, yellow soccer
balls, red cones. Soon there will be work,
love, and children. Here they have each other
to assist, to rely on. Bending and stretching,
cutting and running, hopping from side to side,
they kick the ball toward the net as the goalie rejects
old ideas, new stratagems, oblivious to the roots
of trees pushing up sidewalks or the circling
gulls waiting to congregate on the green field.

Deployment

I make love with my girlfriend before packing.
We fit together like a comma splice. I rush
to fill out the Red Cross paperwork, pick up
traveler's checks, pay the telephone bill,
the electric, the landlord. I remember one
of my drill sergeants, who had been a private
in Vietnam, said pressure is having to cover
your buddies and not having any ammunition.
Everything else, he said, is nothing.

Afternoon

With Playskool mop and broom for oars
you climb into the laundry basket
to sail the green shag sea of the living room.
Ahead lies the Isle of Man. Look
for the place on the beach where the Vikings
launched their raids against Britain, then

came home to build their funeral mounds,
and too where the flotilla of small boats set sail
for Dunkirk, and where I contemplated your birth.
Close ranks with Jack and Jill, your favorite dolls
who have been soldiers and sailors under your
benevolent watch. What are you looking for?

Off your starboard beam, there by the
fireplace, lies the coast of Scotland, near
the blue construction paper waterfall.
Don't set ashore there. Our ancestors learned
scorn for poverty and authority there, and left
their names in the churchyard at Kirkton of Skene.

Keep to port. Encourage your brave crew.
Sail toward the sandy shore of the couch where
I am your personal Neptune, shooing away
the cat shark that circles your ship, sitting
on the stone walls of Peale Castle, scanning
the horizon, awaiting your return, your departure.

Water Listening Device

Stethoscope, resin, fur, rubber tubing, drinking glass, bucket:
by Merritt Johnson, 2016

I'm always wearing red at work,
and I never work alone. There
must be someone with a mop who
rhythmically moves from side to side
or forward and back like a doctor
stitching an eternal wound.
I am most happy when thinking
of Mother and Dad, long ago gone
to floors of buffed marble.
They wanted me to study medicine,
but how could I in this filthy world
where each scratch might fester,
each pinprick poison the blood?
In a sense I am forever treating
the symptoms rather than the causes,
cleaning up grime and carelessness.
Nothing weakens my resolve. Once,
a young man walked by with his mother.
She said, loud enough for me to hear,
"Go to college. You don't want to end up
like him." What does she know of me?
All she sees is this one posture I give
the world. Is one glance enough to judge
an entire life? Sure, late at night, in the dark
of the broom closet, I wonder if things
had been different, if Mom and Dad…
no, why bother? I cannot choose the floor
upon which I am forever about to fall.
A glass half full or a glass half empty
is still half a glass spilled near a crying
child or a parent who may or may not
report it to the manager. Doesn't matter.
I am no caricature of care. Eventually,
I'll be there to help, me, a prophet of
cleanliness, an angel who should have
been at the left hand of Adam, the moment

when God extended his right hand in the
Sistine Chapel and all this mess began.

Baton Rouge

Tonight we're in a church Sunday school room. I'm sitting on a cot as I look at a watercolor painted by a child: "Do this in remembrance of Me"—Luke 22:19 above a brown cross. Whatever I'm supposed to do in remembrance I'm doing. Headquarters is moving tomorrow to an empty Walmart store. A bath in the sink tonight. Holy Bible on the table in front of me. We were handed a Red Cross fact sheet today—"If someone asks you why you aren't in New Orleans, tell them it isn't safe enough and a Red Cross presence might encourage people to return to the city." Yesterday, we were fed pork and chicken, rice and lentil soup, by a Turkish group. That's probably the best Red Cross shelter meal I've ever had. Tonight, we get clotted spaghetti and soggy salad. I'm not complaining. I'm writing.

Cleveland

As I talk about the traffic, she suddenly reaches down
and picks up a gym bag which I hadn't noticed.

She places the gym bag on the bar, unzips it,
pulls out baby powder and sprinkles the bar

with the stuff. What the hell? I think. Then she stands,
steps away from the bar, and uses one foot to slip

off a shoe, the other foot to slip off the other shoe.
She's not wearing socks. She picks up the shoes

and puts them in the gym bag. She unbuttons
her jeans, shimmies out of them, carefully folds

and puts them in the gym bag. She undoes her blouse,
takes it off. She folds the blouse and puts it in the bag,

reaches behind her back with both arms, undoes her bra,
straightens up and places the bra in the bag, too.

She's slender, lithe, and she has my full attention.
She puts the bag on the floor under a bar stool,

and with a practiced grace, she climbs onto the stool,
steps up on the bar, spreads the powder with her feet

before starting to dance. Perhaps she does this
because she likes it, or to support a child, or both.

The memory of her dance returns to me my own youthful body
after a day of driving a truck in the city named after her.

Junking Dream

Dad won't quit. We've already found
a green wooden bench, a belt of nails

for a pneumatic nail gun, and a Mercury dime.
We're in his pickup, parked near train tracks.

He's testing me to see if I am observant,
if I am prepared to ignore fatigue

and do whatever must be done;
what must be done, of course, is always

determined by him. The windshield fogs up,
but he sees something on the other side

of the tracks. Without hesitating he takes us
down a steep grade, then over the tracks

to the other side. Like the gospel song,
at first I am lost, then I am found, or at least

I recognize where we are, near the north
end of Dunton Road where I grew up.

Dad would not have strayed far from home.
We don't find anything else except each other.

A Bureaucracy of Blue Tarps

I ask a guy near Slidell where he rode out Katrina. "Right here," he points to the house behind him. What was it like? "The most terrifying thing I've ever seen. The wind was blowing 150 miles an hour horizontally; then, 30 seconds later, it blew 150 miles an hour from the opposite direction. That's what broke the trees." He is already chain-sawing his way from under the tall pines around his house. A blue tarp covers part of the roof. "Where can I get another one?" he asks, pointing at the tarp. Suddenly the great storm is transformed into a requisition form, the insane wind and rain receding in memory with each movement of my pen.

Ambition

My neighbor screams from
across the street. I stand straight

up, spilling my coffee.
Looking through the window,

I see her hand at her mouth
and her legs bent at the knees

as if the earth were shaking.
I haven't forgotten everything.

Shouldering past my wife,
I run to my neighbor's side

and follow her finger pointing
at the thick black snake

making its way under her car.
Slick as a hawk, I pick it up

by the tail and carry it to the river.
As I casually stroll back to my side

of the street, she waves to me,
a smiling boy again.

On First Looking into Google Earth
after Keats

Little do I travel now that I'm old,
   Though many nice bed and breakfasts have I seen
   When younger, especially on the Isle of Man
Of which travel agents have seldom told.
But my young friends Dawn and Ray hold
   That one doesn't need to take a vacation
   In order to travel to a different destination.
I thought Posh! until I downloaded pure gold
In the Sergey Brin and Larry Page program bold.
   Then felt I like some anime cartoon goddess
With all her horde of eagle-eyed groupies,
   Silent, staring at every wonder of the earth
From Tokyo to Brighton to Perth,
   Except those blocked out for security purposes.

Chain of Command

Jimmy and Rosalynn Carter weave their way to one of the tables. Dressed in a black baseball cap, red bandana, flannel shirt and carpenter's jeans, Jimmy Carter doesn't look like the face I remember on a black-and-white portrait in the hallway of my army barracks, connected with a small chain to portraits of the Secretary of Defense, Harold Brown, the Chairman of the Joint Chiefs, and on down the chain of command, ending with Captain McGill of the 127th Military Police Company. The wrinkles on Jimmy Carter's face surprise me. In that way my father resembles the ex-president, though no one who knows my father would accuse him of smiling too much. Jimmy Carter unwraps his sandwich; the baggies are stamped *A Gift of the American People*. Rosalynn sits across from him, her back to me, a dusty, billowy white shirt topped with a round straw hat, pulled low over her face and neck. She seems unfazed by the heat. "He doesn't mind the pictures," one of the Secret Service agents tells a group of people gathered around. "Just don't interrupt his lunch." Near the front, in a Red Cross jumpsuit, his 110 pocket camera to one eye, my father's scrunched face grins. At that moment he is, as Samuel Pepys described his father in 1666, "one of the most careful and innocent men in the world."

Pink Dogwood

I had no idea the taproot went
so deeply into the dark soil,
that it would cling as tightly
as a thumb in a bowling ball.

I should have stopped digging
when I found the Barber dime.
I should have accepted the coin
as reward enough, backfilled

the soil and left the tree
for the new owners, but the image
of those flawed blossoms
as I worked the shovel and pick

set me to the labor.
In the years to come,
I would look outside
the new bedroom window

and be reminded of the dogwood
cross on Golgotha,
the bleeding hands of Christ
and my own blistered palms.

I watered the dogwood each evening.
My daughter added the tree
to her Now I lay me down to sleep
prayer, along with her grandparents

and her friends from daycare.
Nothing we did could save the tree
from its slow browning.
Now, when I ask my daughter

if she remembers anything
about our home in Kentucky,

she takes off her Beats headphones
and says there were many trees.

Operation Crossroads

The scientists tied the pigs
to the deck at the edge
of the blast zone.
The cameras were set
to run at a thousand
frames per second.
The flash blinded the pigs
before smoke wisped
from their hides, a moment
before the steel heaved
into the pigs' bellies,
before their legs broke.
The scientists used
the word miraculous
to describe the way
some of the pigs
were still alive
the next day when
technicians boarded
the ship to measure radiation.
The eyes of the pigs
had seen the inside of the sun.
Like Shadrach, Meshach
and Abednego,
the pigs lay down
in the fiery furnace.
No golden idol
no sound of the horns
no angel with white wings
before the technicians
cut them open
where they lay,
listened to the static
of the Geiger counter,
recorded their findings,
then dumped them
into Bikini Atoll.

Accident

Jim's answering me as he backs up the ERV. The passenger side rearview mirror just catches a mailbox. We were talking about the Halloween decorations, the ghosts hanging from the low tree branches, what he said to the family of the guy who died in a house fire last week. No damage to the van, though the box now sits parallel to the road. "Oh shit," he says, the most common last two words recorded on airplane black boxes. We step out into the night, and under the gaze of an inflatable witch, I twist the box straight.

Cella

The inner chamber of a temple,
the name of my black and white cat
that argued with me about modernism
and the stock market, she who showed
the way from youth to old age and beyond,
the cat who rewarded me with a mouse
on one of my long ago birthdays
which I let her eat in pure gratitude
and later took her to the veterinarian
for the worms the mouse gifted her,
Cella, whose bump of wisdom
above her left eye grew to unexpected
proportions, the bump she willed to me
over my right eye as a symbol of attachment,
a lesson in my failed study of the sutras,
as something to touch that reminds me
how to love Charlie Parker's "Star Eyes"
if for no other reason than it meant
I was going to scratch her belly for the next
three minutes and thirty-six seconds
which, in a simple declarative statement
like the ones she preferred, is so much
to cherish as to be almost unbearable.

Bondo Billy

Stripped bare as an ingot,
his body reveals its faults.
The mortician applies rouge
and eyeliner, combs gray hair,
folds his arms over his belly
as if he's laughing, something
he rarely did. He might say
the mortician is using Bondo
to cover his flaws as we did
with the 1966 VW we brought
back to life when I was in
high school. That winter,
in the garage heated by
a coal stove, we sanded
and hammered and cut
and riveted that car away
from the junk yard. When
we'd made it as straight
as we could, he spackled
the imperfections with Bondo,
smoothed them with a putty
knife, sanded some more,
and ran his hand over his work.
When the light hit the car
just so, you'd think you were
looking at it through heat
rising from the pavement,
even in January's cold.
There's not another one like it,
he would say. I touch the wrinkles
on his face, tenderly, as I
dare not when he was alive.

Training Torso

Instructor Bracken shows us how we're
supposed to find the xiphoid process
with the fingers of the right hand,
then place the heel of the left on the distal
end, and with both hands at the end of locked
elbows lean into the heart's phantom rhythm.
The practice dummy clicks in protest.
As the old saying goes, if God could have
practiced before creating mankind, he would
have been a Methodist. And it's method
we're learning, our backs rising and falling,
rising and falling, our mouths tasting latex
and disinfectant. Again. Again. Again.

Food Ration Stamps from 1945

The half-empty booklet marks
the end of one privation:
no more packed trains pulling
into and out of the night,
no more sincere exhortations
from local bandstands
to buy war bonds.
Forgotten in a chest of drawers,
the ration book becomes
like a glass vial of morphine,
a reminder of uncertain years
when, from then on,
only the dearth of money,
rather than the war,
dictated how much,
how many, how often.

Welcome to Missouri

Daniel and I run across the closed highway bridges
in the evening. Nine miles of flooded bottomland.
The roof of a gas station. A damaged bridge support.
Flooded train station. And on to the other side of the river,
clouds of gnats, a buzzing and burbling from the bugs
and the water, broken levees, old sandbags, hay bales,
sand frogs, National Guard MPs, the waning moon.

Spitfire

The balsa ribs of the Spitfire's fuselage
seem fragile in my father's hands.

The wings sit drying off to one side:
doped tissue paper, geometry

and glue keeping the pieces together.
Even at leisure a working man seems

to be laboring, his smooth face
unaware of the U.S. Steel strike

of 1958, just months away. Soon,
I will be asking him questions

about ailerons and elevators, dihedral
and lift, distance and endurance.

Sweet Home without Style

> *What we call the beginning is often the end*
> *And to make an end is to make a beginning*
> —T.S. Eliot

Tonight's for remembering
the bitter smell of river mud

on Water Street, the flooded
grain elevators, the uneven

sidewalks, Pam saying yes
when I ask her to marry me.

First thing's a walk to work
in the morning, and the last

a walk home at night. At 11th
and D, an intoxicated man

staggers near. As we come
closer, he asks me if I am OK.

www.ingramcontent.com/pod-product-compliance
Lightning Source LLC
Chambersburg PA
CBHW021159090426
42740CB00008B/1158